PRIMAL VIRTUES

FOR THE

MODERN MAN

JONATHAN RIOS

Psychotherapist

Primal Virtues for the modern man

Printed in the United States of America

First Printing, 2021

KDP amazon

Follow Jonathan on social media:

Website: **www.thriiv.co**

Instagram: Jrios_therapy

Email: Hello@thriiv.co

TABLE OF CONTENTS

INTRODUCTION

The pages before you are not written by a man sitting on the side lines. The words before you are hard earned. As a psychotherapist I've worked with men for nearly two decades. Men of different races backgrounds, and demographics. I've heard their stories. I've lived among them. I've bled with them, cried with them, and been witness to their struggles.

My wife and I have fostered over 12 teenage boys and are currently raising four beautiful daughters. As I write these words I wonder who my daughters will marry and if the men they choose will be worthy of their love. As a father I am concerned about the state of men. I am concerned we have forgotten who we are and what role we have to play.

A spell has fallen over our land. We live in a day of crisis, but you will not hear about it on the 5 o'clock news. Ours is a fatherless generation and a generation without fathers is a generation lost.

Countless men do not know who they are or why they are needed. They had no one to show them the way. They were raised by a loving mother, a school teacher, their peers, and TV sitcoms. In some cases dad was in the home but he wasn't truly present. In other cases his poor example spoiled the vision of what a man can be.

Many have concluded that masculinity equals passivity & niceness or the other extreme- physical dominance through aggression, money, and power.

Many are living lives of quiet desperation. Disillusioned. Angry. Bitter. Tired. They feel forgotten. Unchallenged. Unimportant. Unwanted. The fire has gone from their eyes.

They bounce from job to job, woman to woman, bottle to bottle, podcast to podcast seeking a fix. In search of a remedy for the ache. Out of frustration many have turned to unhindered aggression and exotic expression, or worse, utter domestication.

But what if there was a better way?

If you are reading this book you are likely a man (or a female seeking to encourage your man or son). The virtues set before you are lessons learned through trial and error. They are tried and tested. They are designed as an ethos of sorts. A path towards maturity. A road towards manhood. They are not complex, but they are difficult to uphold as is anything worth striving for.

I implore you. Stamp them on your heart. Memorize them. Allow them to sink in. Put them through the ringer.

If you choose to embrace these virtues, as countless other men have, you will be forever changed. If you find them helpful, I only ask that you share them with the men in your life.

On with the awakening.

Jonathan Rios,

Psychotherapist, husband, father, athlete, outdoorsman.

VIRTUE 1

I AM A WARRIOR I REFUSE TO BE DOMESTICATED

It is one thing to study the warrior lifestyle and another to live it every day. We are the breed who choose to live the warrior creed every day.

In our search for true masculinity, we must come to accept we are designed for war. This battle, however, is one primarily concerned with self-mastery. It is a war against our lesser selves. It is a striving towards nobility and potential. It is a war against selfish desire, passivity,

& undisciplined aggression.

We are seeking a resurrection of the true warrior spirit.

To speak these things in this modern era will immediately draw critique. To call men forward as warriors fills the minds of many with visions of savagery, abuse, and tyranny. The pejorative term often used to describe this type of man is referred to as "toxic masculinity".

What I am proposing is the exact opposite. This is a definitive call for "responsible masculinity". The warrior spirit I am referring to will only make the world a safer place for our children, women, and communities. The true warrior is the one who displays self-control in times of chaos, discipline in the face of excessive abundance, virtue in the face of uninhibited hedonism, and honor in a world of slander and cowardice.

So what does this have to do with you?

Gentlemen, I am calling you to something that transcends Hollywood masculinity. I am proposing that you declare war over yourself. As cultured & experienced as you may be, I am calling you to stand guard over your community. To take responsibility for your business, your wife, your children, your tribe. To patrol the gates and to protect what has been entrusted to you.

But be forewarned. There is an enemy as subtle as the air you breathe. This insidious enemy is called decadence and it is playing for keeps. It's goal is to make you soft and weak through excessive indulgence and luxury. Impotence by way of extreme abundance.

Men, this is our primary obstacle in the pursuit of true masculinity. Softness. Easy living. Sensuality. Passivity.

Before you tune me out consider the following. By the standards of most of the people who have ever lived on this planet, we live like kings. We drive in climate controlled "chariots". We live in climate-controlled houses. We carry cell phones that answer our questions with the push of a button. Fresh water and abundance of food are the norm. We do not hunt our food nor do most of us farm our own lands. Most of us are seldom in any remote danger. Most of us can go days, weeks, or even years without having to exert ourselves physically.

This enemy has taken the fight out of us. Lulled us to sleep. Our souls have shriveled. Many of us are bored beyond measure; and boredom, as we all know, is the devil's playground.

Many of the males I see have grown weak and deformed in body and soul. In short, this thing called decadence has taken the warrior right out of us.

MALE OR MAN?

You had no choice. You were born male. But being born male does not qualify you as a "man" and not all men are warriors either. What makes a man a warrior is his willingness to place himself between what he loves and anything that threatens it. To the warrior honor is everything, it is his driving force. When the warrior holds fast to his creed, he finds he becomes as solid as an oak tree no matter what the circumstances may be.

The warrior comes in many molds, but his core is one of courage. It takes radical courage to stand for the weak or to remain focused when chaos unfolds around you. It takes courage to stand up for truth and justice when they defy popular opinion.

The warrior does not entangle himself with peripheral issues or ego driven debates. He is attentive to his personal responsibilities_and remains resolute towards that which he loves. He is fierce toward his commitments and duties. He is teachable. He is humble. He is brave. He will do whatever it takes to get the job done.

He makes no excuses and owns his mistakes. He need not be exceptionally strong or gifted in martial arts (though he would be wise to grow abundantly in these areas). The warrior understands he must be ready at any moment to defend what he loves. The warrior understands there is a time for rest and a time for action.

The warrior refuses to be civilized & recognizes the cultural drift towards decadence. He understands the inherent dangers of excessive luxury and abundance. He realizes he is the instrument by which protection and provision are sustained, and the instrument must stay sharp and prepared. He is the tip of the spear, always ready in season and out. He understands it is better to be a warrior in a garden than a gardener in a war.

When you finally decide to walk your TRUE path, you will have made an agreement to never be domesticated again. The wild ones, the uncivilized, and the warriors are always rejected among the "domesticated" during times of peace and abundance.

Why? Because they disrupt traditions. They are rough around the edges. They often violate social norms. They aren't politically correct. They aren't subservient to the opinions of the crowd. They aren't manipulated by the threat of rejection or the appeal of applause. The undomesticated are often outspoken towards power structures and anyone who would seek to CONTROL freedoms.

The uncivilized among us offend the sensibilities of others but they are the ones the tribe will always turn to in times of crisis. They are the ones with enough gumption to get the job done.

In times of crisis you don't need "nice men". You need action, boldness, courage. You need dangerous & disciplined men who are capable of great havoc but restrained by virtue.

Most of the "civilized" world fails to fully appreciate the need for savage gentlemen until their airplane is hijacked, and the need arises for courageous and dangerous men to put down the threat decisively. Likewise, the domesticated despise violence until their freedom is at stake & they need courageous men to conquer the beaches of Normandy & stab the enemy through the heart.

When we consider destructive male violence we often think about rape and domestic abuse. We tend to forget about all the "violence" that is currently being done on our behalf to keep us safe from enemies foreign and domestic. Most of us are so far REMOVED from violence, aggression, and pure EVIL that we see no need for warriors anymore. Our detachment has led us to the twisted belief that it is possible to purge this trait from our men all together (or that we should actively shame men for their natural drift towards competition and aggressive release).

We teach young men to "suppress their power, energy, strength, and aggression" by telling them there is something wrong with them. We tell them their aggression is dark, malevolent, & should be ignored and suffocated. We tell them to reject strength and aggression. We tell them to be nice and civilized.

We do this because we fail to understand that aggression and strength are the NEEDED ACTION when evil is at our doorstep. A society that lives in climate-controlled houses, drives in climate controlled cars, and works at climate controlled offices can easily forget that evil and tyranny are always present (while many good men and women are currently fighting hard to protect our security and relative safety).

One day you may need that boy to defend you. If you raise him to be ashamed of his strength and emasculate him he will not be the warrior that is needed in times of crisis. He will be soft and weak and inept. The emasculated men are always the easiest to manipulate and control.

What we do not need are savage brutes who misuse their strength. We need dangerous & disciplined men who have channeled their strength and courage and have cultivated their capacity for aggression so that they are ready and willing when the need arises.

The true warrior is not fooled by the lure of comfort, realizing comfort never made a glorious man. He is well able to enjoy the good things in life and is wise in his dealings while remaining vigilant during times of peace. His goal is peace, always peace. There is a time for peace and a time for war. The warrior knows both and prepares himself during times of peace, ready for action when the moment calls.

There are many forces looking to box the warrior in. So much pressure to CONFORM. The warrior must recognize this and keep his edge. Edges grow rusty when neglected.

This world does not need more domesticated men (or women for that matter)- it needs more trailblazers. More wild men with courage to speak the truth, and more importantly, courage to live it.

We were not born to conform. We weren't born to follow popular culture. We weren't born to succumb to the rat race. We weren't born to bow to perversion and fear. We were born to stand, bravely, as men, wild, disciplined, and free.

VIRTUE 2

I FIGHT FOR WHAT I LOVE UNAPOLOGETICALLY

Ours is a planet at war. We are not in neutral territory friend. Every inch is contested. We are swimming upstream against a strong current.

The dangers of luxury and comfort may lull us to sleep without our conscious awareness. Like the painless bite of a tick, draining its victim of blood and transmitting pathogens that cause disease. There are malevolent forces desiring to neuter, kill, and destroy you and that which you love. Many remain ignorant of this fact, but we are not of that mold.

Our enemies include apathy, fear, deception, greed, ego, cowardice, and anything else that would seek to suffocate our freedoms.

We do not apologize for our aggressive tactics. That which is set against what we love is our enemy. We willingly choose to place ourselves between what we love and the dragons of destruction. We do not neglect our duty but embrace it courageously. Nobility is our friend. It will guide our decisions as we fine-tune our warrior status. Aggressive action against all that is evil is our mandate. We are savage gentlemen carrying nobility in our blood and we make no apologies for that. We will be ready when needed. We do not wait to prepare when the storm hits. We build our ark *before* the storm.

We do not apologize for our beliefs, our sex, our families, our lifestyles, or our goals; assuming of course they align with *Ultimate Truth*. We hold fast to our faith, our loves, our territory with a resolve unlike the common man. We are not common. We will never be common. We, like many of our brothers, choose to be uncommon.

We are not stupid. We recognize that any path we choose will be judged. We have come to realize that standing for what we believe, and what is RIGHT, will incur certain repercussions. We accept that.

We are not amateurs bending to the applause or the rejection of the crowd. We do not fear men, we do however recognize there are things worth fearing. As Plato once said, "courage is knowing what not to fear". We ought to fear living a meaningless life. Cowardice when our loved ones need us to pull through. Apathy when perseverance is needed. Wasting our lives on fleeting pleasures that can't satisfy the soul. Wasting a moment of sleep because we are gripped by the possibility of social rejection (when external opinions were never something we could control anyways).

The fear of God is the spiritual chiropractic adjustment that places all other fears in their rightful place.

If we speak our mind, launch in a particular direction, and hold the line, we may be judged as incompetent, ignorant, insensitive, bigoted, and tyrannical. If we say nothing, appease the crowd, and fail to stand for what we believe, we will be judged as being a coward, a door mat, a people pleaser, a "yes" man, an unimportant, uninteresting statistic.

It is literally impossible to live our lives without judgment from the critic. Our accusers will call us a thousand names. The critic always has something to say. The critic is a coward at heart and must be ruthlessly ignored. We cannot stop to throw rocks at every barking dog. We would get nothing done. Their voices must not be allowed to occupy real-estate in our minds.

We might as well pick our battles wisely and stand unapologetically on our own terms.

COVERT NARRATIVES

I do not write to offend, nor do I write to coddle. I write with sincere concern over the state of our men. When I look around at popular culture today, I see mass confusion, fear, and offended individuals. I hear the repeated echo of two predominate narratives that are destroying men and culture. They are what we might call the machismo narrative & the gender cancellation narrative.

The Machismo narrative goes something like this; To be a man one must stifle his emotions, become stoic. Financial dominance, sexual conquest, and athletic prowess are the pathway to manhood.

Men don't feel, they just DO.

Quit crying. Suck it up. Be a man. Quit acting like your sister.

This narrative is extremely toxic to the male soul, impedes human flourishing, and encourages the lie that malicious aggression, misogyny, and brute force are what it means to be a man. Many young men know no other way. The effect on our daughters, sisters, and wives is egregious.

Equally destructive is the gender cancellation narrative. The narrative goes like this; there is no difference between the sexes. Males and females can do all the same things and play all the same roles. Gender is just a social construct. There is no distinction. Biological markers don't matter. Chromosomes & hormones don't really matter either.

This too misses the mark & belittles the beauty of gender distinction. We have forgotten the beauty of the "other". It is as if, suddenly, the two genders are no longer "enough", no longer mysterious and glorious as they are. We have now decided there are countless genders and pronouns, to which there is no cap.

Distinction does not mean we are unequal, it just means we are uniquely different. The same species but strategically different.

Consider the following analogies. There is a distinct difference in positioning within sport, but each player has a function. To deny function is to destroy the game entirely.

Every soldier performs a unique role in combat. To deny one's role and function places the entire mission in jeopardy.

Wolves hunt in packs, but each member must play their role precisely in order to make the kill.

Each member of an orchestra must play their tune with excellence and respect for the collective. No member of the orchestra is disposable. A pianist is not a drummer. Neither musician is superior. Both are essential & uniquely equipped for the task.

Likewise, in our beautifully complex society women have a distinct role to play, as do men. Their "sound" is unique.

To declare there is no difference in gender & biological function will ultimately create massive confusion. We are already privy to this reality. It is the air we breathe.

Gentlemen, different does not imply gender inequality, it just means we are beautifully & strategically unique. You have a unique role to play. Do not give way to the twisted narratives of the modern era. Your masculine sound is necessary and unrepeatable. We do not apologize for being male. Nay, we celebrate it.

VIRTUE 3

I CHOOSE THE HARD PATH FOR THAT IS WHERE I GROW

Modern men are faced with an interesting question in this era; how much should we indulge in the entertainment and luxury of our time? Compared to our ancestors we live in excessive comfort and abundance. This bubble wrapped existence of the 21st century. Microwave meals, air-conditioned homes, running water, heat, cushy indoor offices, swift transportation, food we don't have to hunt or prepare.

This is a time of extreme *decadence* which is defined as moral or cultural decline characterized by excessive indulgence in pleasure or luxury. The drift toward excessive luxury, abundance, and ease is almost inescapable. We now live in a time where world hunger has taken a back seat to world obesity. That's right, there are more people wrestling with the medical ramifications of obesity then there are people dying of hunger. It's true. Look it up.

This is the era of "faster, quicker, easier" but is "easier" always better?

Should we become like the ancient stoic, keeping ourselves set apart to maintain our independence, preparedness, and masculine ruggedness? Should we take the path of least resistance, or choose the hard path?

Well, that depends. Are you wanting a life of shallow pleasure or deep meaning? You see, masculinity is not, as some suppose, the opposite of femininity. Masculinity, at its core, is the opposite of childhood. To become a man is to leave behind your childish ways. A child is addicted to instant gratification. They want things now. They aren't thinking about the long game. They are thinking of the next sugar hit. They know nothing of responsibility until they are taught. They seek only fun and avoid difficulty.

As men, we must always remember that we have a choice in the matter. When we say "yes" to something we are also saying "no" to something. When we say yes to a late night with the boys, we are likely saying no to an early morning workout. When we say yes to the bimbo at work we are saying no to our wife at home.

When we say yes to countless hours playing Call of Duty what are we saying no to?

When we voluntarily choose the hard path, it is not because we have a desire for pain. We say yes to the hard path so we might meet our potential. We say yes to the hard path so we might be ready in the time of need. So we might be prepared in body, soul, and spirit. "He who sweats most in training bleeds least in battle"- Spartan Warrior Creed, 7th Century.

Muscles don't grow unless stressed. Men don't grow unless challenged. Souls don't grow unless we push them to their limits.

We aren't waiting for challenges to fall into our laps. No. We are actively seeking them with the full knowledge that we are happiest when we see ourselves growing. I repeat, we MUST SEEK THEM OUT.

We must be challenged *physically* through stimulating exercise. The mind is housed within the body. If you desire to have a sound mind, never forget your body is the temple that houses the golden goose. Neglect of the body produces apathy of the worst kind. The challenged body will do wonders for the soul and psyche of a man. Rugged exercise helps us to find release from many of our ailments, anxieties, and agitations. There is deep joy to be found in pushing your body to its limits. To surmount a challenge physically is intrinsically rewarding. To say "I don't like working out" is the mark of a child. Of course you don't like working out. It's hard. It hurts. Maturity requires we embrace things we do not like so we can become who we long to be. After some time we will find our bodies begin to crave the exercise. The body wants to grow in the same way the sword longs to be sharp.

We would also be wise to recognize the reality that fatigue, and low energy will be our constant nemesis. "Fatigue makes cowards of us all" (Gen George S Patton). Low energy & exhaustion will break even the most resilient warrior. Healthy foods, steady exercise, and consistent sleep patterns are a basic foundation for any serious warrior.

We must be challenged at *work*. A man needs to put his hand to something. He needs to exercise his talents. He needs to develop a skill. If he is a janitor let him sweep with excellence. If he is a doctor let him heal with passion. If a man feels unchallenged at work he will need to ask himself: "Have I reached my ceiling in this environment, or must I set new challenges within this environment?" It is his responsibility to seek creative challenges, not his employers. Not all work is a curse. Work is how we provide a service, produce revenue, fine tune our skills, learn how to submit to leadership, and cultivate mental fortitude.

We must be challenged *psychologically*. The mind must be stretched & assaulted with regularity. Set your mind to learn a new subject. Read books that resonate with your soul & stretch your paradigms. Wrestle with philosophy. Tackle deep theology. Intentionally stretch your mind. Begin writing. Drink deeply under the guidance of a wise teacher. Ask more questions. Whatever you do, don't just swallow everything you learn. Don't just believe every podcast you listen to. Contend. Wrestle. Challenge. Repeat.

We must be challenged *relationally*. Lone wolfs never make it. Are you surrounded by lions or sheep? If you desire to be a lion you must train with lions. If you desire to be relationally fulfilled you must surround yourself with men that stoke your fire, call you higher, and speak their mind. Men that aren't afraid to say the hard things. Men that will have your back. You will have to seek them out. They will often be found working hard, flying under the radar, locked in on their targets rather than posting selfies on social media.

We must be challenged *spiritually*. True spirituality is a frontier along the "hard path". It is the call to adventure. It is the call to leave the familiar and launch into the wilds of mystery, tension, and risk. Interestingly enough, three major religions (Judaism, Christianity, Islam) share the historical narrative of a man named

Abraham. He is known as the father of faith. In the story he is told by God to leave his home and country and move into the unknown. He is only told about the general area in which to go, but is not given specifics.

One thing is clear: He is told he must not stay where he is.

With great courage he launches into the great "frontier". This is the way of spirituality. It is the way of humility. It takes great humility to "leave what we know" and move into "unknown realms". If there is a Creator, what is He like? What has He said? What is He now saying? If there is a "voice"" to be heard, how do we hear? Are there others to show us the way?

For many the thought of "organized" religion produces immediate repulsion and holds various negative associations. That is not what I mean.

True spirituality may, or may NOT, be linked to organized religion.

I do not believe organized religions are all bad. In fact, they may be an important part of our lives. However, some organized religions may drain the fire right out of you if you let them. There is often a negative and consistent attitude among the followers of certain organized religions, a judgmental perspective that seeks to tower over others with a false sense of superiority.

True spirituality involves a spiritual connection that produces virtues like humility, courage, hope, peace, love, joy, and honor. You will know a true spiritual person not only by their words but by how they live their lives. Words, by themselves, may be cheap. You shall know a tree by its fruit.

The doorway to vibrant spirituality is always "faith". You can spell faith another way: "R-I-S-K". If you would make moves towards God, you must come to see that He exists and that He rewards those who diligently seek Him. By reward I do not mean a winning Powerball ticket. God, if He exists, is not a genie in a bottle. He is not an idea or a detached "life force" as some espouse. He is the Being that created the universe and the billions of personalities within the human race. That same being created you and you are vital to this planet. You were not born a thousand years ago. You were born for this generation.

We must not allow the excuses of our fathers or the damages of organized religion to deter our pursuit. At the end of the day, every man stands alone before God with no one to point the finger at except himself. Excuses are for children. We are the masters of our own ship. Eternity resides within the heart of men. We may try to suppress it only to find we missed the essential calling of our lives.

VIRTUE 4

I DO NOT DESPISE THE DAY OF SMALL THINGS – THEY PREPARE ME FOR THE BIG THINGS

SON: "Hey Dad"…

FATHER: "Yeah son?"

SON: "Can I take your new truck to the prom?"

FATHER: "Well son, I'd like to let you use the truck but I'm not sure you're ready. Here's the plan. I'll let you drive your mom's minivan for the next 30 days, if you can manage her car well, I'll consider letting you use my truck for the prom".

The son reluctantly agrees to the terms. He drives mom's minivan out of the neighborhood at mach speed, blowing through stop signs, smoking cigarettes behind the wheel, racing down the highway, and leaves his sweaty football gear in the car overnight. Unbeknownst to the son the father is watching him the entire month. He has him followed. He watches as he misuses his wife's not so attractive minivan. After 30 days the son returns excited to use his father's truck. However, the son is not ready for his father's response.

FATHER: "I had you followed all month son. I saw you speeding. The car smells like smoke. You're lucky I didn't call the cops. You were grossly irresponsible and now I cannot reward you with the truck......but........

I'll make a deal with you. I'll give you another 30 days to prove yourself. Drive the minivan as though it was a brand new Lamborghini. Treat it with respect and then come to see me after 30 days."

The son is shocked he's been given a second chance. For the next 30 days he drives it like his life depends on it. He changes the oil, waxes the car, drives the speed limit. He is careful to heed his father's advice. He drives it as though he is being watched. After 30 days her returns. His father smiles, reaches into his pocket and tosses the boy the truck keys.

FATHER: "Great job son. I knew you could do it. You've learned the lesson of stewardship. You've also earned my trust. Enjoy the truck."

To neglect the day of small things is to delay or prevent

your ultimate promotion.

What do I mean by small things? I mean your *current* minimum wage job. Your *current* apartment. Your *current* relationships. Your *current* junkyard car. Your *current* body. Your *current* talent level (or lack thereof)._They ALL MATTER. I can't stress this enough. I plead with you. ALL THE SMALL DAYS REALLY MATTER.

I've had more small days than I can count and I, too, have been tempted to neglect them.

We despise the day of small things for numerous reasons. Many of us do not understand that consistency, hard work, and effort pay off in the end. Many of us have given up on *the process* out of disillusionment and frustration.

The worst thing that can happen to a man is to be

promoted before he is ready. To enter the professional ranks when our skill level is barely on par with the amateurs would be a travesty. To be promoted to the rank of "General" when we can barely fulfill the tasks of a lowly recruit would damage the masses.

Our struggle is real. We long for the day of influence and prominence, and rightfully so (we are created for greatness and glory) but our glory can only be achieved by humility, training, and good stewardship. A house is sustained by a strong foundation. A man is sustained by the foundation of character developed in the hidden days when no one may have been watching. The days when he longed for promotion, did not receive it, and worked hard anyways. When he watched from afar as his friends and family advanced in finances and influence while he fought desperately to suffocate envy and appreciate his meager circumstances.

This of course is not a sexy proposition. This doesn't preach well. No man wants to hear "work hard, embrace hiddenness, and trust the process". Regardless, there are no "hacks" to maturity and development. Muscles do not grow overnight spontaneously. Oak trees take time to grow. Talent and character must be tested and tried to prove their worth. Hold on to the vision. If it wasn't important it wouldn't need to be tested.

I give you this solemn warning: if you choose to neglect small things you will live a life of quiet desperation. Small things grow into big things and you were created for big things. The best time to plant a tree was 20 years ago. The next best time is right now.

VIRTUE 5

I CHOOSE TO LIVE THIS LIFE BY CHOICE NOT BY CHANCE FOR I AM NOT A VICTIM

When we identify as an *oppressed* person we lose. We lose big. Like really big.

Tis true: playing the role of the victim may bring us attention. We may even receive a boost in social status which will mobilize others to come to our defense, but we will have given our "power" away. The thing about victim culture is that it rewards us when we behave as though we are weak, helpless, and owed something. As a therapist I frequently counsel individuals who do not want to be "fixed" because their brokenness brings them attention, money, or security. It gets them noticed and that can feel quite nice when your tank is empty.

Let us be honest for a second, shall we? As a human on planet earth we have it fairly rough. We all experience serious pain at some point in our lives and we are all dying. It's also not too farfetched to say we have all been victimized to some capacity. (Don't tune me out here). Whether that was earlier today when someone cut us off on the highway, or some teenager took a bat to our mailbox. Perhaps a co-worker slandered our reputation, maybe we lost our house to a natural disaster. Many of my clients have experienced rape or physical assault. These are instances of victimization and there are varying *degrees* of severity. We don't need to pretend like these things haven't happened or sweep them under the rug. We must treat each case with the respect and diligence it deserves.

But....

We are also Victimizers. We've slandered others, mistreated others, stolen, lied, abused, neglected, cheated, and misused the things we were responsible for. We have offended others. We've grieved someone at one time or another to varying degrees. We are both Victims & Victimizers. We must understand this before moving forward.

And here's the slippery slope.

Once you begin to see yourself consistently as "the Victim" you will eventually move into a "Victim

Identity". Victim Identified Persons (the wrong kind of VIPs) quickly move into powerless thinking and living and they suffer tremendously because of it.

Victim Identified Persons say to themselves: *"I'm powerless to change. This is my lot in life. I can do nothing to effect circumstances. I'm oppressed, and someone needs to rescue me. I'm incapable. I'm not competent or confident enough to shift things".*

This internal monologue breeds an insidious landscape of resentment, anger, hate, bitterness, jealousy, disillusionment, and hopelessness. This way of thinking becomes a deeply embedded belief system and will affect your behavior drastically.

Is this you? Have you learned the same? Have you been so abused, neglected, and criticized that you've come to believe change is impossible? Are you exhausted from past instances of failure? Are you crushed by years of underlying fear and anxiety?

Don't buy this vicious lie; people change every day. Progress does not happen by chance, it happens by change.

Always remember this... people learn "escape is impossible" through repeated pain and dead-end attempts at escape. We learn this by experience and observation.

We were all dealt a hand in the card game of life and it would be foolish to say life is "fair". Of course life isn't fair. Some of us are living an extremely painful life. Maybe we were dealt a raw hand. That stinks. It's not fair. I'm sorry. I realize what I'm saying is cold comfort.

No need to fake a smile here. I'm not into hype. Let's call a spade a spade. Bill gates is quoted as saying "Life is not fair. Get used to it". Seems like an honest assessment to me.

Here's my question....

What matters now? *How are we going to play the hand we've been given?* Some people choose to look at someone else's hand (comparison), some people choose to quit (suicide, escape through mood-altering substances, or living in a virtual world gaming their lives away), and some people stay in the real game of life and give it everything they've got.

There's a beautiful saying in the Special Olympics: "Let me win. If I cannot win, let me be brave in the attempt". Wow. That's powerful.

What now?

If you find yourself "stuck" in victim thinking, there are a couple steps you need to take to free yourself from it.

Here's your first step. You will have to do something very brave and difficult. You're going to take extreme ownership for the trajectory of your life. You will need to be honest about your dysfunctional belief system and admit that you have been identifying as a victim. Recognize it but don't stay there. Time to stop blaming others. You blaming others is like gasoline to the fire of victim thinking.

Talk to someone, preferably someone who can give you honest feedback; a professional if you have to. Recognize that you are believing lies. You have to allow healthy people to speak into your life and give you constructive criticism. You're going to need insane courage mixed with tremendous humility.

Secondly, grab a piece of paper. Draw a line down the middle. One side should read "Things outside of my control". The other side should read "Things I can control". You'll notice very quickly the list of things outside of your control is very large and extensive and should include other people. You cannot control other people, you really can't. You'll just experience more pain in the end. Things within your control will include your actions, your beliefs, and how you interpret your thoughts.

When we continually focus on things outside of our control we slide into anxiety and worry. We also end up neglecting the things within our control. Hard to do both at the same time.

Third step: Start small, but you need to start taking responsibility for your life. Clean your room. Make your bed. Feed yourself a vegetable (or 5). Floss your teeth. Organize your schedule. Begin an achievable exercise routine. Invest in yourself. You alone are the manager of your own life. Stop expecting your life to "magically" get better because you prayed the right prayer. By all means pray…then get to work!

True meaning in life is directly attached to responsibility.

You'll need to denounce the "I deserve" mentality and convert to an empowered "I'm responsible" mentality. You've got to adopt a belief that says: "I'm responsible to do what it takes to be happy and deeply fulfilled". Stop waiting for God to miraculously zap you with a winning Powerball ticket. "I am responsible" calls us to action. It drives us to go after our dreams and desires. "I deserve" thinking directs us to some external person or power structure to provide something we need. For example, if you tell yourself "I deserve to be happy", that will tend to take the focus away from your responsibility to make it happen and place it on someone else to do it for you.

On the other hand, if you tell yourself "I'm responsible for my own life and happiness", then new and life-giving horizons can open up for you.

Fourth Step: Get some friends. Some genuine friends. Go to a support group. I know this is scary. Good things are behind the scary door. I highly recommend ACA (Adult Children of Alcoholics). Join a church, volunteer, join a sports team, take Jiu Jitsu, join a meet-up group, meet with a therapist. Community doesn't happen by accident. You must be intentional. Remember "I'm responsible for finding some friends" works a lot better than "I deserve some friends". Keep in mind: no community is perfect, some are just like you, some are worse. You've got to extend grace here. There's never going to be a perfect community but there are some really good ones. The world needs you, but you probably don't believe that. It's true. We need you. I NEED YOU. I can't do this alone and neither can you. I repeat, I CANNOT DO THIS ALONE!

Let us be brave in the attempt.

VIRTUE 6

I CHOOSE ACTION OVER TALK, DRIVE OVER MOTIVATION

Deliberate action is the key to unshakeable confidence and effective change. Not good intentions. Not strategies and plans.

This world is in desperate need of men who make less announcements and more assertive moves. In order to do that we must redefine motivation. What is motivation?

Our culture has perverted the definition of motivation by focusing on "feeling".

It has been my observation that many people believe motivation to be "a feeling that spurs action". But feelings are notoriously fickle. We cannot force them. In fact, our attempts to conjure feelings we often "freeze" them. What we see in our day is the sad case of millions of men waiting around for a "feeling" to happen and circumstances to align before they take assertive action.

I see many men seeking motivation (strong feelings and a rise in energy) through YouTube, podcast, books, and inspiring quotes (many of which are amazing), but insufficient as a fuel source.

In my view, motivation is something external. Drive is

the relentless fire within.

It is not until we come to the conclusion that we do *not* require motivation that we can begin to make consistent forward progress. I repeat, WE DO NOT NEED MOTIVATION. Motivation is a farse.

Imagine telling your boss one day: "Sorry boss, I can't make it in for my shift today, I'm not feeling motivated". Real life doesn't work like that.

To help you understand the difference between motivation and drive, allow me to share a personal experience.

Recently, while running a half marathon, I hit a "physical wall" around mile 9. All "feelings to continue running" left the building. The finish line no longer "seemed" important. Energy was low and my knees were screaming for ice. It was the remembrance of my initial goals and values that drove me to finish the race. I had previously determined that I would finish at all costs regardless of pain or exhaustion. I volunteered for the hard path before I began. Why? Because of the joy of completing something difficult. The joy of *surmounting a challenge*.

I knew, from past experiences, that there is little satisfaction when I haven't given my everything. True exhilaration comes through effort and risk. You will rarely find it in the comfort zone.

A man must come to see that the hard path is ultimately the most valuable one. Shallow ponds make for shallow pleasure. To paraphrase the great CS Lewis… Perhaps we are far too easily pleased. We settle for mud puddles because we can't envision what the ocean might be like.

We settle for the easy path because we do not realize there are higher levels of pleasure and fulfillment. The path towards manhood is the path of maturity where we forgo comfort and ease (for a time) so that we may experience deep pleasure and satisfaction and thus move towards our long-term goal of growth and development. The best views atop the mountain require the most difficult climb. The deepest friendships require struggle, grace, and intention. The man who chooses to remain on the couch is the man who will never know the great agony of defeat nor the glory of great victory.

Our calling is to become men fueled by the inner drive of our values, goals, and morality.

VIRTUE 7

I AM RELENTLESS ABOUT THE
TRUTH FOR TRUTH IS NOT WHAT
I WANT IT TO BE, IT IS WHAT
IT IS AND I WILL EITHER
BEND TO IT OR LIVE A LIE

The quote above was coined by Miyamoto Musashi. He was a Japanese swordsman, philosopher, and samurai. Musashi, as he was simply known, became renowned through stories of his unique double-bladed swordsmanship and undefeated record in his 61 duels. As a master samurai who faced death more times than most we would be wise to heed his words.

Truth doesn't care about our opinions. It never cared about our feelings either.

Truth has things to say. Truth is the very thing that establishes order out of chaos. Truth is like a hammer that shatters every rock. We live in a time where truth has become "relative". I hear this phrase all the time… "LIVE YOUR TRUTH"! I appreciate the sentiment and fully support the idea of radical individuality. "Live your life according to what you feel is true-be true to yourself" is the underlying theme of our day but, that is not what I'm talking about when I use the word TRUTH.

I'm talking about living your life in accordance with ultimate truth. Objective truth. Truth that is outside of you and me. Truth that doesn't change due to human opinions and popularity.

Truth is solid. Feelings are fickle.

To rail against THE TRUTH will ultimately destroy you (and those around you). Many men will find at the end of their lives that they lived a life according to their version of "the truth" only to discover their ladder was leaning against the wrong wall. "Your truth" is nothing compared to "The TRUTH".

Here is the truth, men:

- If you live only for selfish gains you will die with serious regret.

- If you rail against moral truth, you will experience inner chaos. (You may have fleeting moments of passion and pleasure, but you will fail to find lasting inner peace).

- If you fail to apply yourself as a protector, provider, and presider (a man who is willing to exercise his bestowed authority and responsibility) you will experience internal angst and wander through life disillusioned by the journey.

When a man rails against the truth there is HELL TO PAY. We see this in nature. The emboldened child attempts to defy gravity by jumping from the tree believing he can fly only to find gravity cared nothing for his "belief". His legs break with ease.

The scuba diver must respect the pressures of the water surrounding him and not ascend too quickly lest he experience the "bends" and die a painful death.

The fire must be kept in the fire place, not in the hallway lest the entire house burn down.

When I talk of "truth", in one sense, I mean ultimate facts (objective truth). In another sense, I mean "moral rules" to live by. Moral rules are like directions. They are instruction for running the human machine, they aren't suggestions. Moral rules are not "take it or leave it" options. When you buy a new car it comes with an instruction manual. To defy the instruction manual spells disaster for the new machine. If you attempt to lube the engine with toothpaste you will not get far. If you attempt to fuel the engine with lemonade the car will not move.

All machines have a function and a purpose. You are

no different.

Automobiles have a function: to get you from A to B, to drive swiftly, but they were never designed to swim oceans. They are designed to perform a function.

The human has a function, a purpose, and many men more educated than I have debated these things for years. If there are ultimate truths concerning the purpose of manhood, what are they?

For starters, you are not a primordial accident. You are not a statistic. You have a part to play in this game. There is an Architect, and you are the designed creation.

The man who believes himself to be purposeless will flounder through life. The man who rejects the truth of a higher power robs himself of a higher purpose. "The fool has said in his heart there is no God" Psalms 14:1.

Like all great works of art that reflect the talent of the painter, your existence on this planet is a call to reflect the ultimate painter. Your value comes by way of the painter's determination, not by the voice of the critic. Some of us have been so busy, distracted by the rat race, so stuck in our pain and fears that we have grown numb to the inner compass, the voice within. It will arise if we can get alone, preferably in nature, in humility, with honest pursuit. The voice may not say what we like. It may disagree with us and our life choices, but the humble man can recognize the call of the architect and bend to the mandates of the instruction manual.

There is a call to something more, but you cannot ascend a mountain and remain at low elevation. You may need to cut some cargo and drop some dead weight. You need not "understand" totally before you begin. None of us do. Did you "understand" the ocean fully before you dove in?

That which is created will never fully comprehend that which is of a higher order. The appropriate response will always be one of awe, wonder, and a humble ear.

VIRTUE 8

MY PAST IS OVER, THERE IS ONLY NOW

Yesterday is dead. It really is. It's dead and over but the truth is many of us are still stuck in the past. Gripped by regret while silently reliving the "glory days" in our minds. The truth is yesterday did happen, but it is now only data stored in our brains and nervous system. This is actually the essence of trauma, frozen memories constantly re-living themselves in the body like the traumatic event is happening now. While some are frozen by fear of the future, others are frozen by regrets of the past. Either will produce neurosis. Think of it like this; most depression exist in the past (we grow sad & disillusioned over what has happened). Most anxiety exist in the future (worried about what might happen & despondent because we can't imagine better days). This is the sad reality for thousands, perhaps millions of people. Stuck in this pathological loop.

But it doesn't have to be this way.

When it comes down to it, the main objective in this life is to really live while we are alive. To accept life on life's terms. To play the hand we've been given as best we can rather than wallow in past regrets. (Equally destructive is to stay frozen in fear over the endless possibilities that the future may present.)

As a therapist, one of the common themes I run into is that of forgiveness. Not of others but of self. When a man forgives himself, hell itself freezes over for he has finally released the burdens that have held him captive for so long. Consider the case of an addict who has violated his own morality and that of his loved ones for the umpteenth time. He often struggles to "release the past". His past becomes his now. Tomorrow is simply ground hog day. He no longer trusts himself. He despairs.

I have also seen many men paralyzed by the phenomenon known as "survivors' guilt". Take the case of a soldier returned from battle as the last surviving member of his platoon. His inner soul is torn. He is confused. "Why did I survive and not them?". Or consider the man caught in an affair. He is remorseful but unable to shake the nagging shame of his betrayal. He believes himself to be "unforgivable".

In my view there is one path to self-forgiveness, I know of no other way. The path toward self- forgiveness is one of radical acceptance. We accept what we did and seek to make amends where possible through restitution. In the case of betrayal, we accept and confess what we did. We admit our wrong whole-heartedly. If we cheated, we confess it and actively seek reconciliation (if it is possible to do so without causing more damage). We actively move towards restitution. If we stole money, we seek to make payments in restitution. As we heed the voice of guilt, seek to make restitution, we find the guilt begins to dissolve. We find our debts are paid. If we have violated our own moral code, we confess it to another human and to God and turn away from such behavior. We may need strong accountability to do so. It does no good to confess and then return to our vomit. This is where we turn towards spiritual strength to carry us through to the light of grace (more on this later).

In the case of survivor's guilt, many find their guilt-ridden grief alleviated through the process of honoring the deceased with a life well lived. In seeking to carry on their legacy through some glorious deed. Some seek to be of great service to others. Many of the soldiers I have counseled found it transformational to ask themselves what their fallen brothers might say to them if they found them wallowing in their guilt. Men aren't formulas, and I don't mean to sound trite, but we would be wise to consider how *honoring* our deceased loved ones might recalibrate the trajectory of our lives.

In the ultimate analysis, we forgive others and accept ourselves not because they/we deserve it, but because we understand that holding resentments against them, or ourselves, will do us no good. It resolves nothing. Our bitterness and self-hatred erode our own souls. Nelson Mandela made the following wise observation: "Unforgiveness is like drinking poison and then hoping it will kill your enemies". What if your inability to forgive yourself is poisoning you? Stunting you? Delaying your breakthrough?

In the same breath we must recognize that we are no better than those who have hurt us. We are not perfect little angels. We are all capable of devastating evil when push comes to shove.

Personally, I have found that I am able to accept myself to the degree that I accept that there is a God and this

God has forgiven me and accepted me into his cosmic family, blemishes and all. (Yes I concede, there is something mystical and sacred about forgiveness that only the forgiven know about). If God can forgive and accept me in my current condition, then I am hard pressed to hold my personal violations against my own soul. His only requirement is that I humbly admit my faults, readily confess my *need*, and receive his forgiveness and unconditional love (come to think of it, my wife has a similar standard). A drowning man may struggle and kick for hours but eventually he must face the grim reality, he can either reach out for help, admit his need, or sink into oblivion.

This is a HUGE barrier for many. They see no need for God (or for the counsel of others who have gone before them). They feel fine just the way they are. They are impressed with their own talent and intellect. They have forgotten the heart can take you places the head can never go.

We are not of that sort. We recognize our need for we have seen our own demons. We have felt enough pain. Of course, we understand why people never stop to look at their own reflection. Reflections reveal the crooked imperfections and past regret. We will never find the light of liberation until we own the darkness within. *"People will do anything, no matter how absurd, in order to avoid facing their own souls. One does not become enlightened by imagining figures of light, but by making the darkness conscious"*- Carl Jung, Psychology and Alchemy

ENLIGHTENMENT

If there is a God, this being is able to do this work of inner liberation because He is able to pardon a vexed soul by whatever means necessary (as long as the soul is willing). Not because the man deserves pardon but because God loves what he has birthed into being. Humans are not valuable because they are wrapped in attractive skin, hold status, or produce millions in revenue. Creatures of God are not valuable because they think themselves to be; they are valuable because the Creator has stamped them with his imprint. Performance and external perfection have nothing to add when it comes to the intrinsic value of a human being.

If these things are true, then it behooves us to recognize our value, the value of others, and the high call placed upon us. We are in fact now confronted by the reality: either take responsibility for this thing called life or neglect the purpose for which we were made. We can never grab hold of our destiny and remain frozen in the past.

We will find in the end that true self-acceptance may only be found by the humble of heart who emphatically recognize their need.

P. K. Bernard was right when he said "A man without a vision is a man without a future and a man without a future will always return to his past". Your past is now data. It happened but it is no longer happening. You must cut the chains. You must move forward. You must take the courageous path. You must treat yourself like you matter. If not you then who? Who will take your place in the game of life? That's just it. There is no one to take your place. You are unique. Unrepeatable. If you don't show up it's not just you who suffers, we all suffer. We all lose.

Yes friend, we are captives to our past by our own choosing. We will either choose the path of self-forgiveness or remain frozen in time. The past is over, there is only now.

VIRTUE 9

IF I DON'T KNOW HOW TO DO SOMETHING, I CAN LEARN HOW

There was a time in your life when you could not ride a bike. You were lacking in the skill until you were taught. There was a time when you could not swim. What happened? You received teaching and thus overcame the obstacle. You became the pupil. If you would be a master at anything in your life, you must first become the student, or as I like to call him, the "fool". The fool is willing to play the part of the idiot until he learns the craft. He understands that he will never be proficient until he subjects himself to the learning process. This is our inherent problem; we believe we ought to be masters from the start. We go to great lengths to avoid looking foolish and thus remain unlearned. We do this because we cannot stand the thought of humiliation and rejection. We think to ourselves "I am not good at this, this must mean I'm incompetent and stupid".

Our fragile ego does not allow us to learn. We think ourselves too old, too young, too stupid, or "above such things". We seek to appear "cool", "collected", and "intelligent". This mindset, however, is the way of pride. Pride, you see, values appearances over actual substance. The wise man is willing to humble himself and lives by these timeless Latin words: *Esse quam videri* *"To be, rather than to appear"*. TO <u>BE</u> RATHER THAN

TO APPEAR!

To become a master at anything mandates that we first become a fool. A student. A pupil. A learner. A doer. A child. A servant. We can learn almost anything if we will give ourselves over to the path of humility. Most of the tasks presented to us are not difficult, they are simply unfamiliar. Once they become more familiar, they will become easier. (This re-frame will work wonders for you if you will adopt it). Our ego's will resist, leaning heavily on fear and intimidation, but we will be ready and waiting to strangle the voice of pride.

Our growth depends on our ability to learn. Our ability to learn depends on our ability to lower ourselves. No outside force can do this for us. Every man must humble himself through many humiliations and trials. Eventually with time we will acquire the skill to which we have applied ourselves if we do not lose heart.

VIRTUE 10

I CHOOSE TO LIVE THIS ONE UNREPEATABLE LIFE WITH INTENTIONS AND GUTS

I've identified the lie of the century and you aren't going to like it.

"You can wait until tomorrow...there will always be more time".

What a load of *bull$#%@!*

Says who?

Who guaranteed you more time? I had the unfortunate

opportunity to learn this lesson early in life. As a 17 year- old I watched my best friend bleed profusely from his brain after a devastating car accident in which I was the driver. I sat there in the grass holding his hand listening to the death gurgle as he lay in a puddle of his own blood. I remember begging God to take my life and let him live. It was traumatic. Shockingly he lived and we are still best friends today. I learned a solemn lesson that day.

This thing called life

 is

short.

It is fragile. There are no do-overs. You get one shot. This isn't some dress rehearsal.

This life is precious. It's unrepeatable. You've got to make it count. You've got to tell the girl you love her. You've got to fight for your family. You've got to go for your dreams. The average American male life expectancy is 76 years old. What the heck are you waiting for?

It takes gumption to live this thing authentically. Raw Courage. Here we are, consumed with fears of social rejection all the while the clock is ticking. At times I run into men who tell me, "I'm not afraid of anything". I simply laugh. The men who say this know nothing about living with courage because they have chosen the "safe path". The path of familiarity. The path where success is guaranteed. Only those who choose to pursue their dreams, take the risk of love, and move into the unknown may know the great triumphs and great defeats of a true hero's journey.

Some of you are thinking: "This guy is being dramatic".
I am not.

Do you know how many people die believing they'd have more time? Do you know how many people die believing they could make restitution or seek reconciliation with those they loved? Do you know how many people die believing they'd have time to make their peace with God only to find they vanished like vapor?

There's an old Hebrew phrase that I took to heart many years ago. I encourage you to learn it.

"Teach us to number our days that we may gain a heart of wisdom" Psalm 90: 12.

That's what we need. WISDOM.

Wisdom to know what to give our time to. Wisdom to know where to pour our energy. Wisdom to know the difference between the good and the best. That's my desire for you. That you would give your life to the things and people that truly matter. Wisdom to know this thing is short and tomorrow is never guaranteed.

The struggle to find meaning in your life may end in madness, tis true, but a life without meaning is no life at all. It will become a life of restlessness, resentment, and vague desire-like a sailboat longing for the ocean but frozen in fear.

Men...IT IS TIME. Take your place, don't wait for life to happen. Go out and stake your claim with all the tenacity and courage you can muster. Launch before you feel ready. Take risks. Fail forward. Dive deep. Lift your sails and ride the winds of destiny wherever they might blow.

You have one unrepeatable life and the clock is ticking. May you be found among those men who never settled for a life of mediocrity. Men who never bowed to the fears of this world.

BIBLIOGRAPHY

1. Holy Bible, New International Version. Zondervan Publishing House, 1984.

2. Jung, C.G. Psychology & Alchemy. Princeton. Princeton University Press, 1968

3. Lewis. CS. Weight of Glory. New York. Harper Collins, 2001

4. Musashi Miyamoto. Book of the Five Rings. Boston. Shambala Productions Inc, 1993

ABOUT THE AUTHOR

JONATHAN RIOS M.S. LICENSED PSYCHOTHERAPIST FL

Jonathan Rios is an athlete turned mental coach and licensed psychotherapist who is deeply committed to remaining undomesticated. He works extensively with addicts, performers, veterans, stay at home mothers, business professionals, and spiritual seekers. He is military academy graduate with a deep appreciation for the warrior ethos.

He currently lives in south Florida with his wife and four daughters. He can be found at Thriiv.co.

Made in the USA
Coppell, TX
09 February 2021